curious about

# MONSTER TRUCKS

BY RACHEL GRACK

AMICUS

# What are you

# curious about?

CHAPTER THREE

**3**

## Monster Truck Events

PAGE

# 14

Curious About is published by
Amicus
P.O. Box 227
Mankato, MN 56002
www.amicuspublishing.us

Editors: Gillia Olson and Alissa Thielges
Designer: Kathleen Petelinsek
Photo researcher: Bridget Prehn

Library of Congress Cataloging-in-Publication Data
Names: Koestler-Grack, Rachel A., 1973- author.
Title: Curious about monster trucks / by Rachel Grack.
Description: Mankato, Minnesota : Amicus, [2023] | Series:
Curious about cool rides | Includes bibliographical references
and index. | Audience: Ages 6–9. | Audience: Grades 2–3.
Identifiers: LCCN 2020001119 (print) | LCCN 2020001120
(ebook) | ISBN 9781645491187 (library binding) | ISBN
9781681526850 (paperback) | ISBN 9781645491606 (pdf)
Subjects: LCSH: Monster trucks—Juvenile literature.
| Truck racing—Juvenile literature.
Classification: LCC TL230.15 .K64 2023 (print) |
LCC TL230.15 (ebook) | DDC 629.224—dc23
LC record available at https://lccn.loc.gov/2020001119
LC ebook record available at https://lccn.loc.gov/2020001120

# CHAPTER ONE

# What are monster trucks?

Monster trucks are huge trucks with giant tires. Most have wild paint jobs. Some look like animals or popular characters. They perform **stunts** at events. Most of all, fans love watching monster trucks fly through the air!

**Grave Digger performs a huge jump at a Monster Jam event.**

# What is the most popular monster truck?

**Grave Digger has ghosts and a graveyard painted on it.**

Grave Digger is a Monster Jam favorite. It has a spooky paint job and red headlights. This truck goes all out during **freestyle** events. Its wild stunts rev up fans. Grave Digger likes to bury the competition. It has more wins than any other!

ZOMBIE

DRAGON

EL TORO LOCO

MEGALODON

MAX-D
(MAXIMUM
DESTRUCTION)

# How big are monster trucks?

Monster Mutt
Dalmatian and
Megalodon race to
cross the finish line.

They stand 12 feet (3.7 m) tall and are just as
wide. Some weigh 12,000 pounds (5,443 kg).
That equals two regular pickup trucks. Everything
they do is big! They jump over other trucks. They
can get 35 feet (10.7 m) off the ground.

# What kind of tires do monster trucks use?

**Crew members check on Monster Mutt Dalmatian after an event.**

Early trucks used heavy farm machine tires. Today's trucks use specially made tires. A tire and wheel weighs almost 645 pounds (293 kg). Each tire is 5.5 feet (1.7 m) tall. That's taller than you!

## DID YOU KNOW?

Monster truck tires can cost over $2,500 each. A truck can go through 8 tires in a year.

# Do monster trucks have big engines?

Oh yeah! Their engines are twice as big as a regular pickup engine. They put out 1,500 **horsepower**. These powerful machines can hit 100 miles per hour (161 kph). They are custom built and cost $50,000.

A monster truck engine is huge! It's four to five times more powerful than a pickup engine.

# CHAPTER THREE

# What are monster truck events?

At events, monster trucks compete. Pairs of trucks race over dirt tracks. Drivers show off wild skills. They do stunts to earn points. Drivers pull **wheelies** and whip **donuts**. They do backflips and make crazy jumps. The truck with the highest score wins the event.

**Monster Jam's Dragon can shoot fire!**

**Backflip: a complete 360-degree flip.**

**Stoppie: a truck balances on its front tires.**

**Cyclone: spinning in one spot really fast.**

**Sky wheelie: a truck "stands" with its front tires in the air.**

The Monster Jam truck does a backflip over Son-uva Digger.

# What's it like in the stands?

It's loud and exciting! Monster trucks roar into the **arena**. The sound of the powerful engines fills the air. Many fans wear earplugs. They cheer and wave signs. They go wild after a daring stunt.

### DID YOU KNOW?

There has been a Monster Jam event on every continent except Antarctica.

Driver Krysten Anderson gets strapped into Grave Digger.

# What's it like behind the wheel?

It takes monster skill. Drivers flip the power switch and press the gas pedal. They steer the front and back tires separately. All the while, the truck is bouncing around. Drivers have little time to think. They drive by feel!

# What happens in the pits?

**Pit crews** fix the trucks. Monster trucks take a beating at every event. Crews must work fast. They make repairs. They change giant tires in a few minutes. A new engine takes just two hours.

A pit crew fixes Zombie so the truck can compete in the next event.

# STAY CURIOUS!

## ASK MORE QUESTIONS

**Where can I find a monster truck event?**

**How do you build a monster truck?**

**Try a BIG QUESTION:**
**How can I become a monster truck driver when I grow up?**

## SEARCH FOR ANSWERS

**Search the library catalog or the Internet.**
A librarian, teacher, or parent can help you.

**Using Keywords**
Find the looking glass.

**Keywords are the most important words in your question.**

**If you want to know about:**
- where to watch monster trucks, type: MONSTER TRUCK EVENTS
- how a monster truck is built, type: MONSTER TRUCK ENGINEERING

## FIND GOOD SOURCES

### Here are some good, safe sources you can use in your research.
Your librarian can help you find more.

### Books

**Monster Trucks** by Matt Doeden, 2019.

**Monster Trucks** by Thomas K. Adamson, 2019.

### Internet Sites

**Monster Jam: The Making of Megalodon**
*https://www.monsterjam.com/ en-US/videos/making-megalodon*
Monster Jam creates and promotes monster trucks and events. Watch their video to learn how Megalodon was made.

**Monster Jam: Freestyle Highlights World Finals XX**
*https://www.monsterjam.com/en-US/ videos/freestyle-highlights-world-finals-xx*
Monster Jam is the most popular monster truck organization. The World Finals are the top competition.

Every effort has been made to ensure that these websites are appropriate for children. However, because of the nature of the Internet, it is impossible to guarantee that these sites will remain active indefinitely or that their contents will not be altered.

## SHARE AND TAKE ACTION

### Talk to a parent about going to a monster truck event.
Some events even let you help judge!

### Want to drive a monster truck someday?
Check out Monster Jam University. Learn what it takes to drive a monster truck. *https://www. monsterjam.com/en-US/news/ behind-scenes-monster-jam-university*

### Design your own monster truck.
Draw it and then tell someone why you chose that design.

# GLOSSARY

**arena** A large area used for sporting events.

**donut** A trick where a vehicle drives in a tight circle.

**freestyle** An event in which competitors are able to use different styles or methods to win.

**horsepower** A unit used to measure the power of an engine, based on how much a horse can pull. An average-sized car has about 120 horsepower.

**pit crew** The members of a monster truck team who repair the truck.

**stunt** An unusual or difficult trick.

**wheelie** A trick where vehicles drive only on their back wheels and the front wheels are off the ground.

# INDEX

## About the Author

Rachel Grack has been editing and writing children's books since 1999. She lives on a ranch in Arizona. Hot cars have always fired her up! At one time, she even owned a street rod—a 1965 Ford Galaxie 500. She loved cruising with the windows down. This series refueled her passion for cool rides!